# HINDSIGHT

## 20/20

# MAURY

# DAVIS

### TEN MISTAKES THAT OFFER
### CLARITY AND VISION

STUDY GUIDE

# HINDSIGHT

## 20/20

# MAURY

# DAVIS

## TEN MISTAKES THAT OFFER

## CLARITY AND VISION

AVAIL

# CONTENTS

# I Micromanaged Gifted People

"*Delegating saves time, empowers staff, and allows the organization to work more efficiently. You can't manage the high-level vision while you're constantly in the trenches trying to do everyone else's job for them.*"

# READING TIME

Read Chapter 1: "I Micromanaged Gifted People" in *Hindsight 20/20*; reflect on the questions and discuss your answers with your study group.

Do you think delegation is important in the workplace? Explain your answer.

_____

_____

_____

_____

_____

_____

_____

What do you think are the effects of micromanaging? Are they positive or negative?

_____

_____

_____

_____

_____

_____

# REFLECT ON

Acts 1:6-9 (NIV)

*"Then they gathered around him and asked him, 'Lord, are you at this time going to restore the kingdom to Israel?' He said to them: 'It is not for you to know the times or dates the Father has set by his own authority. But you will receive power when the Holy Spirit comes on you; and you will be my witnesses in Jerusalem, and in all Judea and Samaria, and to the ends of the earth.' After he said this, he was taken up before their very eyes, and a cloud hid him from their sight."*

Why did Jesus entrust flawed people with His ministry?

_____

_____

_____

_____

_____

Where did Jesus say their power would come from? For what purpose?

_____

_____

_____

_____

_____

Have you ever been micromanaged? How did it make you feel?

_____

_____

_____

_____

_____

What are the differences between discipleship and micromanagement?

_____

_____

_____

_____

_____

_____

What's your perspective on failing? Explain your answer.

_____

_____

_____

_____

_____

_____

_____

What are the advantages of trust in the workplace?

_____

_____

_____

_____

_____

_____

_____

_____

Why is delegation so essential to the fulfill-ment of your high-level vision?

_____

_____

_____

_____

_____

_____

How can micromanaging inhibit the gifts of others?

_____

_____

_____

_____

_____

_____

Do you think delegation with trust can empower others? How so?

_____

_____

_____

_____

_____

# I Stopped Pursuing Formal Education

*"Leaders make the best decisions when there's a blend of intuition, information about risks and rewards, advice from gifted people, and intentionality to deliver the desired outcomes."*

# READING TIME

Read Chapter 2: "I Stopped Pursuing Formal Education" in *Hindsight 20/20*; reflect on the questions and discuss your answers with your study group.

How do you feel about education? Do you aspire to learn?

_____

_____

_____

_____

_____

How do you discern what's true from what's false?

_____

_____

_____

_____

_____

# REFLECT ON

**Hosea 4:6 (NIV)**

*"Because you have rejected knowledge, I also reject you as my priests; because you have ignored the law of your God, I also will ignore your children."*

What do you think is God's expectation of our education?

_____

_____

_____

_____

_____

Can biblical knowledge enhance your relationship with God?

_____

_____

_____

_____

_____

Can education lead to higher job performance? Is this always the case?

_____

_____

_____

_____

_____

When making decisions, which is more important, intuition, or information?

_____

_____

_____

_____

_____

_____

*"The most successful people in the world are filling their minds with the ideas and theories of experts in the field without ever leaving a room."*

Do you think it's important for leaders to adapt?

_____

_____

_____

_____

_____

How can challenging mindsets and assumptions lead to growth?

_____

_____

_____

_____

_____

Why is it important to develop a filter?

_____

_____

_____

_____

_____

Do you have an ultimate source of truth?

_____

_____

_____

_____

_____

How can knowledge of history affect the future?

_____

_____

_____

_____

_____

# I Was Insensitive to People's Feelings

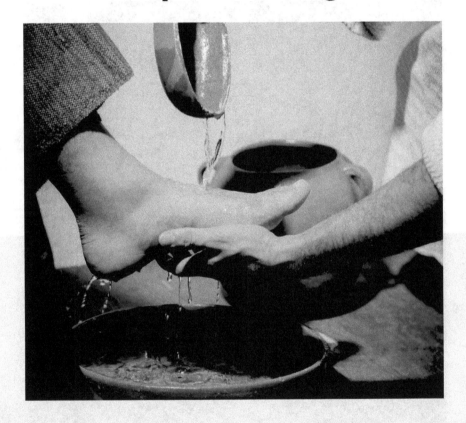

*"Jesus always treated people with the utmost respect—those who ridiculed Him, those who didn't understand Him, and even those who hated Him. He didn't run over them to accomplish His mission ... they were His mission!"*

## READING TIME

**Read Chapter 3: "I Was Insensitive to People's Feelings" in *Hindsight 20/20*; reflect on the questions and discuss your answers with your study group.**

Are you aware of how you affect the feelings of those around you?

_____

_____

_____

_____

_____

_____

Have your feelings ever been hurt in the workplace? Was the situation eventually addressed?

_____

_____

_____

_____

_____

_____

# REFLECT ON

**Psalms 139:13-14 (NIV)**

*"For you created my inmost being; you knit me together in my mother's womb. I praise you because I am fearfully and wonderfully made; your works are wonderful, I know that full well."*

Why is it important to recognize that we are wonderful creations of God?

_____

_____

_____

_____

_____

Do you see the brilliance of God's design in others, or just you? Explain your answer.

_____

_____

_____

_____

_____

How can a positive emotional atmosphere affect the workplace? What about a negative atmosphere?

_____

_____

_____

_____

_____

Describe self-awareness in your own words. Why is this important to practice?

_____

_____

_____

_____

_____

How are your relationship management skills? How could they improve?

_____

_____

_____

_____

_____

_____

_____

What does respect mean to you? How do you practice this in your relationships?

_____

_____

_____

_____

_____

_____

How can you make those close to you feel loved and encouraged?

_____

_____

_____

_____

_____

_____

_____

What are the differences between self-awareness and social awareness? Which do you need to work on more?

_____

_____

_____

_____

_____

_____

_____

_____

Do you sacrifice people's feelings for performance in your organization?

_____

_____

_____

_____

_____

_____

Take time to reflect on your past week. What could you have done differently keeping people's feelings in mind?

_____

_____

_____

_____

_____

_____

_____

# I Confused "Authentic" with "Unfiltered"

*"All leaders should master words—their meaning, their intent, their reception, and their inflection. If you can control words, you can motivate people and enact real change."*

## READING TIME

Read Chapter 4: "I Confused 'Authentic' with 'Unfiltered'" in *Hindsight 20/20*; reflect on the questions and discuss your answers with your study group.

What does it mean to be authentic? Who in your life would you label authentic and why?

_____

_____

_____

_____

_____

_____

Why is it so important for leaders to be authentic?

_____

_____

_____

_____

_____

# REFLECT ON

**Ephesians 4:29-30 (NIV)**

*"Do not let any unwholesome talk come out of your mouths, but only what is helpful for building others up according to their needs, that it may benefit those who listen. And do not grieve the Holy Spirit of God, with whom you are sealed for the day of redemption."*

Why do you think it is important to filter what we say?

_____

_____

_____

_____

_____

What do you think this passage means when it refers to "unwholesome" talk?

_____

_____

_____

_____

_____

What are some of the negative results that come from being unfiltered?

_____

_____

_____

_____

_____

Do you consider yourself authentic? How does what you say line up with what you do?

_____

_____

_____

_____

_____

How can leaders benefit from a mastery of words?

_____

_____

_____

_____

_____

_____

_____

What is the big difference between being authentic and being unfiltered? Which do you look for in a leader?

_____

_____

_____

_____

_____

_____

_____

How can you be authentic within your organization?

_____

_____

_____

_____

_____

_____

_____

# I Made Bad Staffing Decisions

*"Each person has a unique motivational style, unique talents, unique experiences, and unique dreams."*

Read Chapter 5: "I Made Bad Staffing Decisions" in *Hindsight 20/20*; reflect on the questions and discuss your answers with your study group.

What do you think is the most important aspect of a new hire?

_____

_____

_____

_____

_____

_____

What do you expect out of new employees? Explain your answer.

_____

_____

_____

_____

_____

_____

# REFLECT ON

Luke 10:1-4 (NIV)

*"After this the Lord appointed seventy-two others and sent them two by two ahead of him to every town and place where he was about to go. He told them, 'The harvest is plentiful, but the workers are few. Ask the Lord of the harvest, therefore, to send out workers into his harvest field. Go! I am sending you out like lambs among wolves. Do not take a purse or bag or sandals; and do not greet anyone on the road.'"*

What stands out to you about this passage?

_____

_____

_____

_____

_____

Explain why Jesus delegated. Why is this so important in ministry?

_____

_____

_____

_____

_____

_____

How can the over-expectations of a new hire cause chaos?

_____

_____

_____

_____

_____

Do you think it's important to let people fail? Why or why not?

_____

_____

_____

_____

_____

_____

Why is it so important to take time in the hiring process?

_____

_____

_____

_____

_____

_____

How do you motivate? Does a one-size-fits-all approach work when it comes to motivation?

_____

_____

_____

_____

_____

_____

How can you work to develop and grow new staff?

_____

_____

_____

_____

_____

_____

Explain the phrase: "Trust, but verify." Do you think this is effective?

_____

_____

_____

_____

_____

Why is it important to hire to the culture of your organization? How can you do this?

_____

_____

_____

_____

_____

Explain the benefits of being familiar with your staff's leadership love languages.

_____

_____

_____

_____

_____

# I Was Politically Divisive

*"Blending truth and love is essential; and to communicate them well, we need to understand how the hearer interprets our words."*

## READING TIME

Read Chapter 6: "I Was Politically Divisive" in *Hindsight 20/20*; reflect on the questions and discuss your answers with your study group.

Which comes first: your politics or your faith?

_____

_____

_____

_____

_____

_____

Do you think politicizing Christianity has positive or negative effects? Why?

_____

_____

_____

_____

_____

_____

# REFLECT ON

**James 1:26-27 (NIV)**

*"Those who consider themselves religious and yet do not keep a tight rein on their tongues deceive themselves, and their religion is worthless. Religion that God our Father accepts as pure and faultless is this: to look after orphans and widows in their distress and to keep oneself from being polluted by the world."*

Explain the passage. What is religion according to James here?

_____

_____

_____

_____

How can you keep yourself from being polluted by the world?

_____

_____

_____

_____

Why is it important to put Christianity before politics?

_____

_____

_____

_____

How can associating a political stance with Christianity result in limited outreach?

_____

_____

_____

_____

_____

What is the difference between your primary purpose and your primary passion?

_____

_____

_____

_____

_____

_____

_____

In your own words, describe what happens when you speak truth without love.

_____

_____

_____

_____

_____

_____

In your own words, describe what happens when you speak love without truth.

_____

_____

_____

_____

_____

_____

What are the advantages of empathizing with others?

_____

_____

_____

_____

_____

Why is it important to target everyone in ministry? Explain your answer.

_____

_____

_____

_____

_____

# I Didn't Listen to Advice

*"Listening to advice often accomplishes far more than heeding it."—Malcolm Forbes*

# READING TIME

Read Chapter 7: "I Didn't Listen to Advice" in *Hindsight 20/20*; reflect on the questions and discuss your answers with your study group.

Do you ask for advice often in your life and ministry?

_____

_____

_____

_____

_____

How can advice be advantageous amidst uncertainty?

_____

_____

_____

_____

_____

# REFLECT ON

**Proverbs 27:5-6 (NIV)**

*"Better is open rebuke than hidden love. Wounds from a friend can be trusted, But an enemy multiplies kisses."*

When a close friend or family member gives you advice, do you tend to listen?

_____

_____

_____

_____

_____

Are you quick to accept advice from an enemy? Explain why not.

_____

_____

_____

_____

_____

Are you quick to heed advice from those close to you? Why or why not?

_____

_____

_____

_____

_____

How can advice be advantageous? How can it be harmful?

_____

_____

_____

_____

_____

_____

What are the main qualities you look for within an advisor?

_____

_____

_____

_____

_____

_____

_____

Why is collaboration so important? How can you seek to collaborate on more projects within your organization?

_____

_____

_____

_____

_____

_____

Define active listening. How can active listening change your operation?

_____

_____

_____

_____

_____

_____

_____

How does a reconciling environment benefit an organization? What can you do to assist in the creation of this environment?

_____

_____

_____

_____

What kind of work do people produce when they recognize that they are valued?

_____

_____

_____

_____

Why is filtering advice so essential?

_____

_____

_____

_____

chapter 8

# I Didn't Celebrate Others' Wins

*"What matters is how I treat people today—the impact
I make on their hearts as well as their performance.
Celebrating people isn't optional equipment for
leaders; it needs to be standard on every model."*

## READING TIME

Read Chapter 8: "I Didn't Celebrate Others' Wins" in *Hindsight 20/20*; reflect on the questions and discuss your answers with your study group.

How often do you encourage others around you?

_____

_____

_____

_____

_____

_____

_____

How important do you think encouragement is in ministry and the workplace?

_____

_____

_____

_____

_____

_____

# REFLECT ON

**Hebrews 3:12-14 (NIV)**

*"See to it, brothers and sisters, that none of you has a sinful, unbelieving heart that turns away from God. But encourage one another daily, as long as it is called 'Today,' so that none of you may be hardened by sin's deceitfulness. We have come to share in Christ, if indeed we hold our original conviction firmly to the very end."*

According to the passage, why is it so important that we encourage those around us?

_____

_____

_____

_____

_____

How can you "share in Christ"?

_____

_____

_____

_____

_____

How do you actively show gratitude to those around you?

_____

_____

_____

_____

_____

How can you celebrate people and their achievement more intentionally within your organization?

_____

_____

_____

_____

_____

_____

Why are assumptions dangerous, especially regarding encouragement?

_____

_____

_____

_____

_____

_____

Why is it important to know people's motivational buttons?

_____

_____

_____

_____

_____

_____

_____

Why does celebrating people need to be a leadership standard?

_____

_____

_____

_____

_____

_____

_____

Reflect on the past week. What is an easy way to express gratitude to someone who did a great job?

_____

_____

_____

_____

_____

chapter 9

# I Didn't Take Enough Time to Think

*"When we're too busy, we don't take time to quiet our hearts to really listen to the Holy Spirit. A settled soul is responsive instead of reactive."*

## READING TIME

Read Chapter 9: "I Didn't Take Enough Time to Think" in *Hindsight 20/20*; reflect on the questions and discuss your answers with your study group.

Do you think it's important to take time off?

_____

_____

_____

_____

_____

_____

_____

How can working non-stop affect you?

_____

_____

_____

_____

_____

# REFLECT ON

**Philippians 4:4-9 (NIV)**

*"Rejoice in the Lord always. I will say it again: Rejoice! Let your gentleness be evident to all. The Lord is near. Do not be anxious about anything, but in every situation, by prayer and petition, with thanksgiving, present your requests to God. And the peace of God, which transcends all understanding, will guard your hearts and your minds in Christ Jesus.*

*Finally, brothers and sisters, whatever is true, whatever is noble, whatever is right, whatever is pure, whatever is lovely, whatever is admirable—if anything is excellent or praiseworthy—think about such things. Whatever you have learned or received or heard from me, or seen in me—put it into practice. And the God of peace will be with you."*

Why is it so important to surrender our issues to God?

_____

_____

_____

_____

_____

What sticks out most to you in this passage?

_____

_____

_____

_____

_____

What are your priorities? Have they shifted since you have started in the ministry?

_____

_____

_____

_____

_____

Why is keeping priorities straight so important? How can you practice this?

_____

_____

_____

_____

_____

_____

Why is reflection essential to any operation? Explain your answer.

_____

_____

_____

_____

_____

_____

_____

Why can a lack of delegation be destructive?

_____

_____

_____

_____

_____

_____

_____

How can uninterrupted work cloud the original goal?

_____

_____

_____

_____

_____

_____

_____

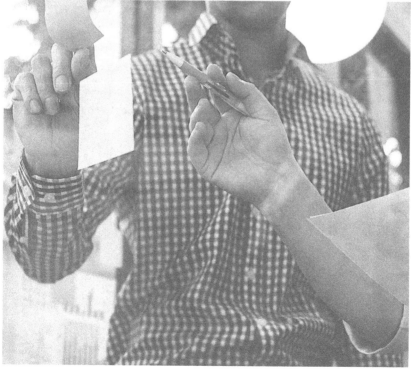

What are some ways you can incorporate rest and reflection into your life?

_____

_____

_____

_____

_____

Why is keeping a focus on the future important?

_____

_____

_____

_____

What's the difference between being responsive and reactive?

_____

_____

_____

_____

_____

# I Stayed Stuck in Old Ideas

*"One of the primary roles of leaders is to tailor their message to a changing culture. If they don't keep their eyes open, they won't keep up with the change, and they'll become irrelevant."*

## READING TIME

Read Chapter 10: "I Stayed Stuck in Old Ideas" in Hindsight 20/20; reflect on the questions and discuss your answers with your study group.

Do you think it's important for leaders to adapt?

_____

_____

_____

_____

_____

_____

_____

Explain what you think it means to be relevant. Does your organization live up to this definition?

_____

_____

_____

_____

_____

_____

_____

# REFLECT ON

**Hebrews 5:8-14 (NIV)**

*"Son though he was, he learned obedience from what he suffered and, once made perfect, he became the source of eternal salvation for all who obey him and was designated by God to be high priest in the order of Melchizedek. We have much to say about this, but it is hard to make it clear to you because you no longer try to understand. In fact, though by this time you ought to be teachers, you need someone to teach you the elementary truths of God's word all over again. You need milk, not solid food! Anyone who lives on milk, being still an infant, is not acquainted with the teaching about righteousness. But solid food is for the mature, who by constant use have trained themselves to distinguish good from evil."*

Explain what sticks out to you about this passage.

_____

_____

_____

_____

_____

Why do you think it's so important to be familiar with the "teach-
ings about righteousness"?

_____

_____

_____

_____

_____

How can adaptation change the effectiveness of an operation?
Explain your answer.

_____

_____

_____

_____

What are some of the effects of not changing with the times?

_____

_____

_____

_____

_____

What are some of the ways your organization can adapt?

_____

_____

_____

_____

_____

How can you challenge your ways of thinking?

_____

_____

_____

_____

_____

What can your organization do to remain effective amid crises?

_____

_____

_____

_____

_____

How can you keep an open, but rooted mind to the future change that is sure to come?

_____

_____

_____

_____

_____

CPSIA information can be obtained
at www.ICGtesting.com
Printed in the USA
BVHW070039110522
636630BV00013B/1571